Helping Hands

At School

Ruth Thomson

WAYLAND

First published in 2006 by Wayland,
an imprint of Hachette Children's Books

Editor: Laura Milne
Managing Editor: Victoria Brooker
Senior Design Manager: Rosamund Saunders

Design: Proof Books
Commissioned photography: Chris Fairclough

Additional photography: Thanks are due to
Coleridge Primary School for kind permission
to reproduce the photograph on page 6.

British Library Cataloguing in Publication Data:

Thomson, Ruth
Helping hands at school
1. Schools – Juvenile literature 2. Teachers – Juvenile literature
I. Title II. At school
371.1'02

ISBN-10: 0-7502-4855-6
ISBN-13: 978-0-7502-4855-6

Printed and bound in China

Hachette Children's Books
A division of Hodder Headline Limited
338 Euston Road, London NW1 3BH

Acknowledgements
The author and publisher would like to thank the following people for their help and participation in this book: the staff, parents and pupils of Coleridge Primary School, Crouch End, London, particularly Shirley Boffey, Paul Sibson, Jamie Breuer, Isabel Richert, Jayne Saunders, Bet Spencer, Jean Linden, Michael Hooper, Paula Poplar, Sylvia Laguna, Makida Smith, Adrian Hardy, Sue Fage, Louisa Munro, Paul Baker, Sheela Sakhabuth, Christine De Souza, Emily Holmstoel and PC Pamela White of the Metropolitan Police Force, London.

Contents

Words in **bold** can be found in the glossary.

Our school

We work at a primary school. The school has 470 pupils and more than 50 staff.

Some of the staff at the school ▼

The school is **surrounded** by trees and shrubs. Most classrooms open on to one of the four separate playgrounds.

▼ Children in the playground

The head and deputy head

We are the head and the deputy head. We make sure that the school runs well. We have meetings with staff and parents.

▲ We often meet to plan things.

◀ I greet children and parents in the morning.

▲ Sometimes, I give out awards to children who have behaved especially well or done good work.

The classroom teacher

I teach a class of Year 2 children. We follow a **timetable** of lessons. Every day we do reading, writing and maths.

I have time each week to plan new lessons. ▶

Today the children are learning about rhyming words. ▼

Once a week, we have circle time. Today the children are talking about what makes them feel happy or sad in the playground.

Being a good speaker and listener

When you speak:

- Look at the person you are talking to.
- Speak clearly and loudly.
- Let other people join in.

When you listen:

- Look at the speaker, keep still and follow what they say.
- Wait for your turn to speak.

At circle time everyone takes it in turns to speak. ▼

Classroom assistants

We are classroom **assistants**.
We move around the
classroom helping children.

I help the children get ready for a play they will be doing in assembly. ▼

I wash up and put away **equipment**, such as paint pots and brushes. I also help put up displays of the children's work.

▲ I help the children with their painting.

◀ I am a **special needs** assistant. I work with only one child in a class.

Art and music teachers

I am the art teacher. I have arranged a collection of African **sculptures** and **fabrics** in a classroom.

I ask children to look carefully at the shapes, colours and patterns. ▶

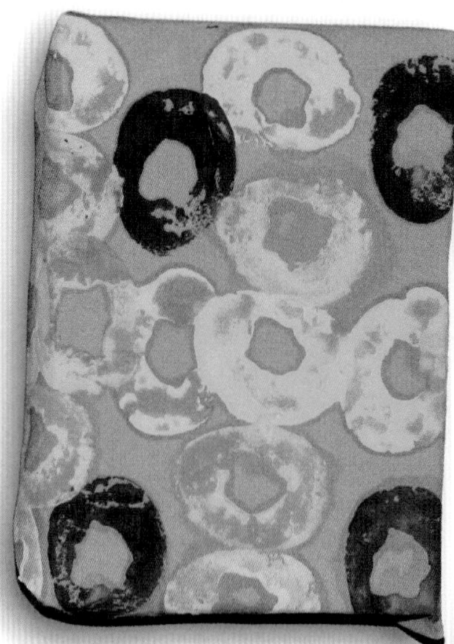

◀ The children's art is displayed on walls around the school.

I am the music teacher. I teach music to everyone in the school.

▲ I play my guitar to help the children keep in time.

◀ These children take turns to make up a tune on the **glockenspiel**.

Office staff

We work in the school office. We have all sorts of jobs to do.

I greet visitors. ▶

I answer the phone and take messages. ▼

I have done a course in **first aid**.

If children feel ill or hurt themselves, they come to me for help. ▶

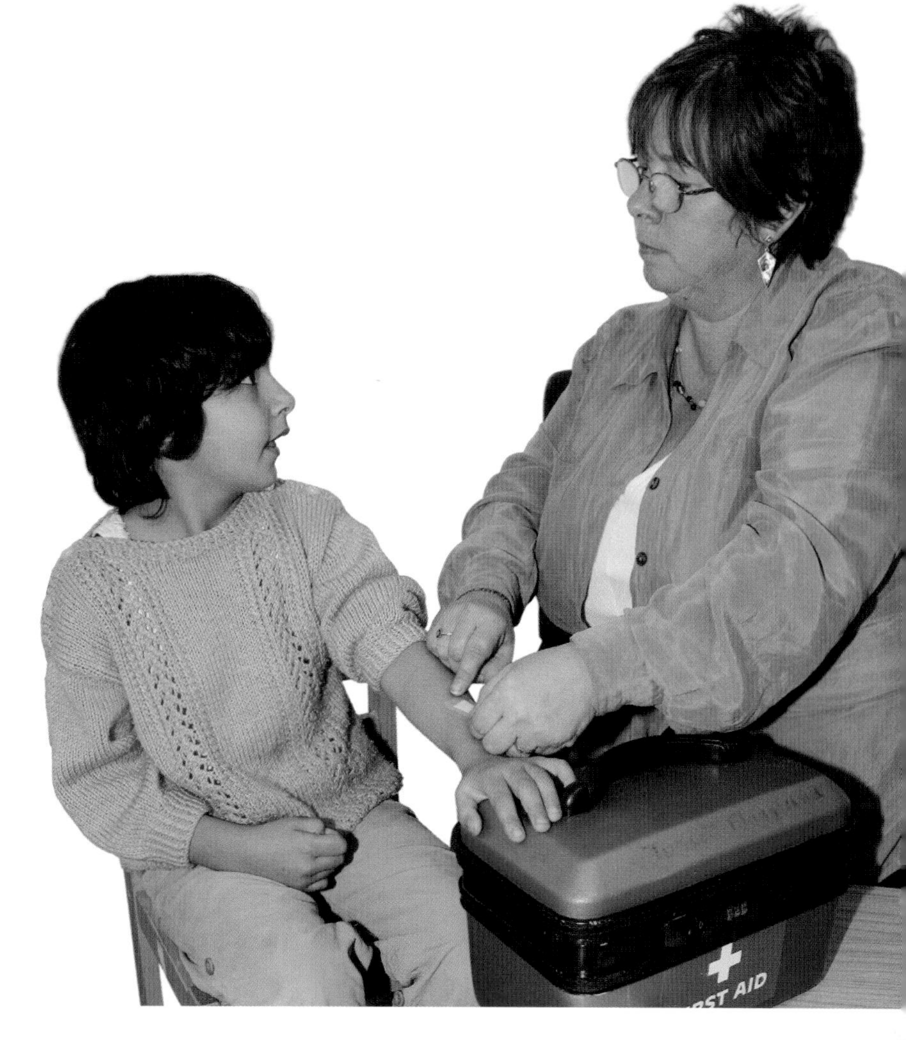

I order all the **stationery** for the school. ▼

The site manager

I am the site manager. I look after the school building and grounds.

After school and at weekends, I sometimes repaint the classrooms.

▲ I change lightbulbs and mend broken **equipment**.

I keep the playgrounds and paths tidy. ▼

Early every morning,
I unlock the school and
let the cleaners in.

I open the school gates
to let in the children.

▲ The cleaners
make the school tidy.

The school crossing patrolman
helps the children cross safely. ▼

School cooks

We cook meals for the children in the school kitchen. There is a different **menu** every day, with a choice between fish or meat and a **vegetarian** dish.

◀ We prepare the dishes that need cooking in the oven.

▼ We make fresh salad every day.

There are two sittings for lunch. The children queue up and we serve them.

Eat a mixture of food to work and play well

* Growing foods: meat, fish, eggs, lentils, beans
* Grains: rice, pasta, noodles, bread, cereal
* Milk foods: cheese, yogurt and milk
* Fruit and vegetables

▲ A school meals assistant helps serve the food.

The children

We take it in turns to be **helpers** for our class. Two children are helpers each day.

▲ We tick the register on a whiteboard.

We pick up all the hoops at the end of playtime. ▶

We are in Year 6. We have been trained as 'bus-stop **buddies**'. There is a pretend bus stop where children can go if they are feeling sad at playtime.

◀ We help any sad children to feel better, and help sort out any arguments.

Parents

Many parents help in the school. Some help in class. They listen to children reading or cook cakes and biscuits with small groups.

▼ I listen to children reading.

Some parents run school **clubs**.

I run an organic gardening club. This week I help the children clear away fallen leaves. ▶

I run a dance club. I teach the children dance routines. ▼

School visitors

All sorts of people visit the school. Once a year, a nurse gives the children eye and hearing tests. Sometimes **actors** visit and perform funny musical shows.

▲ I lead the school **orchestra**. We practise once a week.

▲ I am a police officer. I talk to children about how to keep themselves safe.

Glossary

actor a person who acts a part in a play

assistant a helper

buddy a friend

club a group of people who meet regularly to do a shared activity

equipment all the things you need for a particular job or activity

fabric a woven material, like cloth

first aid treatment of a sick or hurt person before a doctor arrives

glockenspiel a musical instrument with a row of different-sized wooden or metal bars, which are hit to make notes

helper someone who assists or gives support to somebody else

menu a list of food to eat in a café or restaurant

orchestra a large group of musicians playing together

rules instructions about what you are allowed or not allowed to do

sculpture a piece of art that is modelled or cast, like a statue

special needs assistant a person who works with children that need extra help

stationery paper, pens, crayons and other things you use for writing or drawing

surrounded on all sides

timetable a chart listing the time and day when lessons will happen

vegetarian food that doesn't contain meat or fish

See for yourself

Compare your own school with the one in this book. Interview people who work at your school about their job.

Here are some questions to get you started:

- What does your site manager do?
- Who makes your school meals?
- Who teaches art, music and sport?
- What **clubs** does your school offer? Who runs them?
- How do children help one another?
- How do parents help at school?
- Who makes visits to your school?

Children made up these rules:

Class rules

* Follow directions.
* Keep your hands, feet and objects to yourself.
* Do not leave the classroom without permission.
* Be kind to others.

- What rules does your school have?

Index